Little House, Big Trip

A guide to
Laura Ingalls Wilder homesites

Words and Photos by
Gina Parsons

Copyright © 2017 Gina Parsons

All rights reserved.

ISBN: 152347372X
ISBN-13: 978-1523473724

For my sweet Lindsay. What wonderful adventures
we've had on the prairie and beyond!

CONTENTS

	Introduction	Page 1
1	Big Little House Trip Is On	Page 3
2	Choosing Where to Stay	Page 6
3	Camping Out Vs. Staying in a Hotel	Page 9
4	When to Visit	Page 12
5	Planning the Trip	Page 14
6	Building an Itinerary	Page 18
7	Pepin, Wisconsin	Page 21
8	Independence, Kansas	Page 27
9	Walnut Grove, Minnesota	Page 31
10	Burr Oak, Iowa	Page 42
11	De Smet, South Dakota	Page 47
12	Mansfield, Missouri	Page 58
13	Other Sites of Interest	Page 64
14	Tips for a Great Little House Trip	Page 65

INTRODUCTION

The cool water washes over my feet, and the pebbles crunch under my waterproof sandals. I hold out a hand to my 8-year-old daughter Lindsay, who steps hesitantly into Plum Creek.

"Are there any leeches?" she asks one more time. I assure her that there aren't any, although earlier we did see one swimming around farther upstream. I'm pretty sure that by now it has floated downstream from where we are. Anyway, we were visiting Plum Creek in Walnut Grove, Minn. to see the Laura Ingalls Wilder homesite. Having leeches attach themselves to our legs in this creek would be a great part of the adventure, right?

I first read a "Little House" book when I was in third grade. I received paperback copies of "Little House in the Big Woods" and "Little House on the Prairie" for Christmas. I loved those books and borrowed the others from a friend to read. I also watched and loved the TV show. After I grew up, I didn't think about Laura very much. But when my son was young, I bought the complete "Little House" book set for a couldn't-pass-up price. I reread the books and fell in love with them again. I've read them all every couple of years since then.

When she was old enough, I began reading the books to Lindsay, and she became hooked on Little House too. One day, she asked if we could visit the places where Laura had her adventures. I said no, but then I pulled out a map and started thinking, why not? In 2013 we took a two-day trip to visit our closest Laura site – The Laura Ingalls Wilder Museum in Mansfield, Mo. After that trip I really wanted to take a bigger trip and visit the four main northern homesites in Iowa, Wisconsin, Minnesota and South Dakota. In summer 2014, we were able to do that, plus in the fall, we took a separate trip back to Mansfield and continued west to the Laura homesite near Independence, Kansas.

Here is the story of our journeys. My goal is to provide tips and information that will help you on a Little House homesite tour of your own, or make you feel like you've visited the sites. But I hope you find it entertaining too.

I've tried to be as accurate as possible, but I apologize if any information was left out, or has changed.

A note, you may notice that I didn't include the name of every place where we ate and stayed. I did that to avoid dating this guidebook, but also I don't want to appear to recommend any particular business over another. I feel our one experience with a business shouldn't sway or dissuade anyone from patronizing it. I recommend checking reviews from multiple travelers on websites to determine where to stay and eat.

Now grab your sunbonnet and climb into the covered wagon as we head out!

1. THE BIG LITTLE HOUSE TRIP IS ON

When I realized a week-long summer trip to the northern Midwest homesites was feasible, I began to plan. I decided which sites we would visit, and in what order. It wasn't too difficult since the towns are pretty much laid out in a loop to our north. We began the trip in Burr Oak, Iowa, our closest northern homesite. The next stop would be Pepin, Wis., then Walnut Grove, Minn., and finally De Smet, S.D. I liked this because other than Burr Oak, which wasn't mentioned in the Little House books, we would be going in the order of the books. We visited Mansfield, Mo., and Independence, Kan. on a separate trip.

Dressing the part: finding prairie clothes
Once I decided we were going on the big homesite tour, I wanted to find Lindsay the perfect prairie dress to wear for the Laura Look Alike Contest in Walnut Grove, and of course, just to wear while we were there. The gift shops at each of the homesites sell pioneer clothes, but I didn't want to spend the time on our trip shopping for a dress. If I knew how to sew, I would have made the dress myself. But I've never made anything more complicated than a pillow, so I had to find someone else to make the dress.

I first looked on store racks for modern clothes that could stand in for pioneer clothes. I did find a couple of sundresses that looked somewhat Laura-like, but I wasn't satisfied with those for the Laura Contest. I looked on eBay, but everything I found was either the wrong size (usually too small), or not the right look. I also was unable to find a local tailor who could make an entire dress, and I thought that option would be too expensive anyway.

I searched online, trying to find someone who made historic dresses. I found one dressmaker who makes "modest" clothes, which looked very much like Little House-type dresses. The price was fairly reasonable. I decided to order. Lindsay and I looked at the swatches of fabric on the computer screen, and made our choice. It was March, and our trip was in July, so it seemed like there would be plenty of time. But before placing the order, I called the dressmaker to verify how long it would take to receive the dress. She said she was fairly behind and that we could expect to receive the dress in 8-10 weeks. That meant it could be as late as June before we received it. I didn't want to wait that long.

My internet searches found another dressmaker, one who specializes in historic and costume dresses. A phone call to her revealed she could have a dress to us within a week of placing the order. The dress was slightly more expensive than the other dressmaker, especially since I planned to surprise Lindsay by ordering the matching dress for her American Girl doll, but I reasoned that since the trip itself was relatively inexpensive, I could splurge on this item. Lindsay and I looked at the styles, and chose the pioneer girl dress style. The dress had a Peter Pan collar, and a full skirt. It came with a white apron, and a bonnet that matched the dress. I asked for a couple of modifications: short sleeves because I expected it to be hot during our trip, and no lace on the collar, because Laura would not have had fancy lace.

A week or so after I ordered it, the dress arrived, and it was perfect. Lindsay was excited to dress like Laura, and she was happy the doll would match her on our trip. The next weekend, Lindsay and I drove to a nearby city-owned log cabin. When we got there, she slipped the pioneer dress on over her street clothes, and posed for photos.

Wearing the perfect prairie dress.

On our trip, she put the pioneer dress on right before the Laura contest in Walnut Grove. She then wore it for the next few days. She wore it while she waded in Plum Creek, to the pageant that evening, and she wore it for the day and a half that we were in De Smet. She also wore it as a costume at Halloween. It was well worth the price.

2. CHOOSING WHERE TO STAY

On our first night, we would be in the Burr Oak, Iowa area. I originally planned to reserve a hotel room, but the rate was more than I wanted to pay. Fortunately Lindsay thought camping and sleeping in a tent would be fun, so I decided that's what we'd do. I compared the camping options in Burr Oak and also looked at the campgrounds to the north in Lanesboro, Minn. Staying in Lanesboro would be a little farther drive after a long day of driving, but it would put us closer to our goal of Pepin on Day 2.

I debated if I would be too tired to drive the 30 to 40 minutes north to overnight in Lanesboro, or if we should backtrack 20 minutes south to Decorah. I finally chose Decorah because Lanesboro appeared to be a more popular destination for campers and so I reasoned would be more crowded. Ultimately we stayed at Pulpit Rock Campground, the city-operated campground in Decorah. It was very pretty, and there was plenty of open space on the Wednesday evening we were there. I don't regret the decision, but it wasn't as tranquil as I expected. People in an RV talking around their campfire, plus noise from the highway made it hard to sleep.

To give us a break from nights of camping, I wanted to stay in a hotel on the second night. The plan was to wake in Decorah, drive to and visit Pepin, then travel west toward our next stop of Walnut Grove. I was happy to find a hotel with a small indoor waterpark in Owatonna, Minn. Owatonna is about halfway between Pepin and Walnut Grove, so it was a perfect location.

On our third and fourth nights, we would be in Walnut Grove. The Plum Creek Park campground in Walnut Grove is just down the road from the pageant grounds. The campground begins taking reservations on Jan. 2 for campsites for days in June, July and August, plus Memorial and Labor Day weekends. I called on Jan. 2 to make our reservation, and was excited to receive a paper copy of the reservation confirmation in the mail about a week later in an envelope decorated with a line drawing of Walnut Grove sites. That took care of nights three and four.

For our fifth night on the road, we would be in De Smet. I debated whether to stay in a covered wagon at Ingalls Homestead, or pitch our tent there. Truthfully, I wasn't sure that I wanted to stay in the covered wagon. First off, I was afraid it would feel like we were spending the night in a big box, and that I would feel claustrophobic. I also felt the price was a bit high. But then I imagined being there. I pictured Lindsay peeking out of our tent that we'd already slept in for three nights and asking why we weren't staying in a covered wagon.

So on a cold morning in February, I called the Ingalls Homestead in De Smet and reserved the last covered wagon available for that night. Five months later I was happy for several reasons that we stayed in a wagon. It was windy and would have been hard to put up the tent, and chilly that night, but cozy in the wagon. And of course, it was a unique experience. We both loved the novelty of staying in a wagon.

Our sixth night on the road was a wild card. We would either stay in a tent at Ingalls Homestead in De Smet, or if we were ready to leave the area, I had found a hotel in Sioux Falls, S.D. where we could stay. It had a pool with waterslides, plus great ratings on online websites. I called and found that they had plenty of rooms, and they'd likely have rooms available without making a reservation. As it turned out, we were ready to head out of De Smet after the one night, and we did stay at the hotel in Sioux Falls.

So when choosing where you want to stay, take into account what kind of place you prefer. As I'm writing this, none of the homesite towns have chain hotels, and certainly none have luxury hotels. If that is what you prefer, you'll need to stay farther away from the homesite town.

Again, I recommend checking reviews from many travelers on tripadvisor.com and other travel websites to determine which place to stay would be best for you.

3. CAMPING OUT VS. STAYING IN A HOTEL

As already noted, all of the homesites are located in small towns that have few lodging options. Personally, I'd rather camp in a tent than stay in an overpriced motel, but obviously that is a matter of opinion. If you have an RV, you may want to travel and stay in it. Lacking an RV, camping will mean staying in a tent. Here are pros and cons of tent camping.

Pros:
Experiencing life similar to (though certainly not exactly like) pioneer life. You're going on this trip to see where Laura lived her adventures, right? Why not stay in what's essentially a mesh log cabin?

Pulpit Rock Campground in Decorah, Iowa, is located next to the Upper Iowa River.

Price. Camping in a tent will save you money. Even if you buy a brand new tent for the trip, the price of staying in a tent is much less expensive than staying in a hotel.

Availability and location. In a few of the towns, there are more campground options than hotels. In Walnut Grove, Plum Creek Campground is only a mile or so from town, and a quarter of a mile from the pageant. In De Smet, the Ingalls Homestead is on the homestead grounds, and half a mile from the pageant.

Back to nature. Tent camping makes it easy for you to get back to nature. Everything is right outside your door. If you want to throw a Frisbee disc, or see the river, it's just a pull of your zipper door away.

Cons:
Tent set up and take-down. This is a big negative for me. Putting the tent up, and taking it down takes time away from your vacation, plus let's face it, it's a hassle. To speed up the set up/take down process, be sure to practice set up and take down before your trip.

Noisy neighbors. Granted, if the walls are thin, you can hear your neighbors in a hotel or bed and breakfast. But when you're in a tent, the walls are mere mesh, so you will absolutely hear everything that happens nearby. In Walnut Grove, we endured the loud music of our RV neighbors both during the day and at night. In Decorah, and one night in Walnut Grove, people talked loudly around the campfire until late into the night, making it difficult for us to sleep.

Safety. Before our trip, I had never camped at a campground and was concerned that we might be a target for thieves or worse. My online searches about camping safety uncovered no instances of people causing harm to campers. On the trip, I never felt unsafe. Still, I stayed aware of our surroundings, and was vigilant about keeping our valuables locked up, or with me.

Using public restrooms. No explanation is necessary, right? And if flush toilets are important to you, check that the campground has them. One privately-owned campground near Decorah does not have flush toilets.

Exposure to the elements. If it rains a lot during your stay, you and your stuff will likely get wet.

Lack of electricity. You probably take charging your mobile devices and camera batteries for granted. You'll always be able to find an electric outlet, right? If you're camping, don't count on it. At the campground in Decorah, the restroom was too far away for me to comfortably leave my phone to charge. I recharged in the car as we drove the next day.

At Plum Creek Park Campground in Walnut Grove, I had planned to plug my phone into an outlet in the restroom. However, after leaving the phone plugged in for more than an hour in the morning, I found that my phone was barely charged. Either it wasn't a powerful outlet, or the electricity was going off and on (which it did occasionally even while I was in the restroom). So at the festival in Walnut Grove, I had to plug my phone into an outlet in a park pavilion so that I would have enough battery power to take photos of Lindsay in the Laura contest. If I camp in Walnut Grove again, I'll upgrade the reservation to an RV camp spot that has electricity.

One other note, the covered wagons at Ingalls Homestead in De Smet have electrical outlets. Ours worked very well, charging both camera and phone batteries. The Wi-Fi there was super too.

4. WHEN TO VISIT

All of the sites are open during the summer so that makes it a great time to plan a tour. On the last three weekends in July, Walnut Grove and De Smet each have pageants. Walnut Grove performs on Friday and Saturday evening, De Smet performs on Friday, Saturday, and Sunday evenings. So you can go to Walnut Grove's pageant one night (or two!), and the De Smet another night.

Fall also can be a good time to visit. The Mansfield museum has its one-day Laura festival in September, and also a pageant for several weekends in the summer and fall. The Pepin museum has a one-day Laura festival in September. The Little House on the Prairie museum in Independence, Kansas has its festival in June.

If you do plan a visit for the spring or fall, be sure to check that the site will be open. All of the homesites close in the fall, and reopen in the spring. So if you visit during the winter, you will not be able to go inside the museum buildings at any of the sites. Check the website of the homesite you want to visit for the most up-to-date open dates. Do note, the museum in Mansfield and the "Farmer Boy" site in upstate New York usually each host a one-day Christmas event in December.

To visit during special events or not
When choosing when to visit, you may want to find out when events will take place at the homesite, and plan your visit to coincide with the events. The crowds at most events are not excessive in my opinion, and visiting during an event will let you see something – perhaps a pageant or a festival – that you wouldn't ordinarily see.

We took our trip to the northern sites on the second weekend in July, the first weekend of the pageants in Walnut Grove and De Smet. At each of the homesites we visited, a moderate amount of people milled about. It wasn't an overwhelming amount, just enough to make us feel like we weren't the only people who love Laura.

5. PLANNING THE TRIP

Trust the Ingalls family to settle in out-of-the-way places. Not one of the "Little House" sites is near an interstate highway. That means that getting there will probably take longer than you expect. For at least part of the journey to each site, you'll be driving on roads with only one lane in either direction. And particularly in the northern sites, you'll have to slow down as you drive through small towns. And that RV in front of you, driving 55 miles per hour? Just try to get around it on busy Highway 14 in Minnesota during the summer.

> **By the numbers: distances**
>
> Burr Oak, Iowa to Pepin, Wis. – 93 miles; about 2 hours
>
> Pepin, Wis. to Walnut Grove, Minn. – 193 miles; about 4 hours
>
> Walnut Grove, Minn. to De Smet, S.D. – 118 miles; about 2 ¼ hours
>
> De Smet, S.D. to Independence, Kan. site – 572 miles; about 9 ¼ hours
>
> Independence, Kan. site to Mansfield, Mo. – 199 miles; about 3 ½ hours

But even if you live outside the Midwest, it is possible to visit all of the Midwest sites in one trip. You could fly to Minneapolis, and make a big loop, going southeast to Pepin and Burr Oak, then southwest to Mansfield, further west to Independence, back north to De Smet, east to Walnut Grove, and back to Minneapolis. Or you could visit the northern Midwest sites in one trip, and catch the Mansfield and Independence sites on a separate trip.

Whichever route you take, know that you'll need more travel time than the amount given by map websites. As noted earlier, you'll be driving on rural state two-lane roads. So when you get stuck behind a slow driver, you're driving slow too. When you drive through a town, you have to slow to the lower speed limit. Map websites apparently assume that you're driving 80 miles per hour the entire time.

You might wonder if you need to visit each homesite. I'll say each is unique. If you're a Laura fan, they are all worth visiting at least once. That said, we skipped Spring Valley, Minn., where Almanzo's family settled after they left New York state. Getting there would have taken at least two hours from time at other sites, and the museum has no items Laura owned. We also passed by Vinton, Iowa, where Mary attended the Iowa College for the Blind. It would have taken a couple of hours from the time we had to spend in Burr Oak.

We also have not visited the Almanzo homesite in New York state. The visit for us would require an airplane ride plus several hours of driving. Hard to justify for just one site, but I'm hoping we'll get there some day.

We have not visited any of the cemeteries in homesite towns. Many people like seeing that piece of history, but I don't. I'd much rather see where people lived, than see their final resting place.

My two cents about the cost

Of course, a trip to see the LIW homesites isn't free, but when compared to most other vacations, the price is extremely reasonable. Hotels (where available) are on the lower end of prices. If you stay at a campground, the price is quite low. Tent camping rates range from around $10 a night at Ingalls Homestead in De Smet, SD, $15 a night in the city's Pulpit Rock Campground in Decorah, Iowa; $20 a night in Plum Creek Park in Walnut Grove, Minn. Food also is inexpensive, partly because there aren't many upscale options. I saw quite a few campers cooking their own meals in both Walnut Grove and De Smet, which presumably would keep the cost even lower. Currently admission to the homesite museums ranges from $3 for the Little House on the Prairie museum in Independence, Kansas, to the highest at $14 for adults, $7 for children at the Laura Ingalls Wilder Home and Museum in Mansfield, Mo.

Gift shops

For Lindsay and me, buying items in the gift shops was an important part of our trip. I couldn't resist buying books about Laura that I'd never seen before, and unique Laura souvenirs (who doesn't want a covered wagon pencil sharpener with Walnut Grove's unique Laura logo on the side?). In general the prices were reasonable especially when compared to most (every) tourist place you visit. For instance, two weeks before our trip, we visited our local zoo. A small water globe at the zoo was $10. In Walnut Grove, the LIW water globe was $4.50. How could we resist? I reasoned that we were spending so little on the trip itself, I could splurge in the gift shops.

Charlotte dolls.

Here is a know-before-you-go tip. Each homesite carries its own version of the Charlotte doll – that precious rag doll that Laura received as a Christmas gift in "Little House in the Big Woods." I planned to buy Lindsay whichever version she wanted. You could collect them all as you go, but if you plan to buy only one doll, you might want to check out the dolls on the websites of the homesites before you visit, and see which you like the best. They are all cute, but Lindsay chose the $30 version in Walnut Grove, our third homesite on the trip. She thought it looked closest to the description of the doll in the book. The doll even has a "Handmade in Walnut Grove" patch sewn onto it. Who doesn't want something handmade at a Laura homesite town?

I loved seeing Lindsay clutching her own rag doll Charlotte as we completed our trip. She played with the doll quite a bit after we came home, and still loves her.

6. BUILDING AN ITINERARY

For our summer trip to the northern Midwest homesites, we began at our home just west of St. Louis, Mo. on a Wednesday morning. To help with your own plans, here is our trip itinerary. For the most part, we were able to stick to the itinerary I'd planned.

Our trip itinerary
Day 1: Left home at 7:45 a.m., drove north to Burr Oak, Iowa, arrived at about 2:30 p.m. Toured museum, looked around and bought gifts at gift store. Drove south to Decorah, Iowa, checked in at campground at about 5 p.m. Set up tent. Drove to downtown Decorah to pick up supper. Ate supper, looked at river and played with a flying disc at the campground. Went to bed at about 10 p.m.

Day 2: Left campground at 9:15 a.m., after grabbing breakfast to go, headed north on Highway 52 toward Pepin, Wis. Arrived in Pepin, 11:15 a.m. Visited museum and gift shop. Ate lunch at Pickle Factory about 12:30 p.m. Walked on beach and marina until 2 p.m. Drove to wayside where we looked at log cabin, took photos. Left about 3:15 p.m. headed for Owatonna, Minn. Drove north on Great River Road, crossed river at Red Wing. Drove on Highway 61, then Highway 19, then Interstate 35 to Owatonna. Arrived about 5 p.m. Ate fast food supper, played in hotel's mini-waterpark until about 9 p.m. In bed at about 10 p.m.

Day 3: Left hotel about 11 a.m. after spending morning in hotel's mini-waterpark. Visited a small reptile zoo. Left Owatonna at 1:30 p.m. after fast food lunch. We visited the Sod House on the Prairie near Sanborn for about a half hour. We arrived in Walnut Grove about 4:30 p.m. Checked in at Plum Creek campground, set up tent. Got pizza at convenience store and ate supper. Played in campground open area. Went to pageant grounds at 7:30 p.m. Pageant began at 9 p.m. After pageant, we met actors and got autographs. Arrived back at tent at 11:45 p.m.

Day 4: Left campgrounds at about 9 a.m. Ate breakfast at Nellie's Place. Arrived at museum at about 9:45 a.m., ahead of the rush. Toured museum buildings. Left by 11 a.m. Walked to festival in town square. Looked at and bought items vendors had for sale. Lindsay did crafts. Ate lunch we'd ordered from the convenience store. At 1 p.m. Lindsay changed into her prairie dress to prepare for Laura look-a-like contest. Lindsay did more crafts. More photo opps. Contest began at 3 p.m. Contest was over at 4:45 p.m. Drove around town. Saw (and heard) Pa's bell in church tower. Drove to dugout site. Waded in creek, took photos at dugout site. Left dugout site at 6:30 p.m. Drove back to town and got supper. Ate at campsite. Played in open area. At 8 p.m. went to pageant site. Watched pageant. Back at camp at 11:30 p.m.

Day 5: Left camp at 9:45 a.m., headed for De Smet, S.D. Arrived in De Smet at 12:20 p.m. Picked up lunch. Went to Ingalls Homestead and checked in. Ate lunch. Toured the homestead, and did activities there. At about 4:30 p.m. we checked into our covered wagon. Went into town to get supper, ate in covered wagon. Drove to pageant grounds at 7 p.m. Pageant began at 8 p.m., ended at 9 p.m. Returned to wagon for bed.

Day 6: Until 10 a.m. did activities on homestead grounds we'd missed the previous day. Went to museum, bought tour tickets. Did activities in Discovery Center. Took 11:30 a.m. tour, which ended at about 1 p.m. Visited Loftus store. Left De Smet at 1:30 p.m. We arrived at the hotel in Sioux Falls at about 3:30 p.m.

The only thing I didn't account for was time for Lindsay to sleep late in the morning. We returned to the campground at nearly midnight on the two nights we were in Walnut Grove. That, coupled with being in an unfamiliar place and not sleeping well at night, meant that she slept in every morning. Waking her was a struggle, which meant we started our days later than I'd planned. Still, we did almost everything I had planned.

In October of the same year, we took a weekend trip to Mansfield, Mo., and Independence, Kan. For that trip, we left home in the St. Louis area on Friday at about 7:30 a.m. and drove to Mansfield. We stopped at Baker Seed Company for lunch, and arrived at the homesite at about 1 p.m. We left the homesite at about 4 p.m., then stayed the night in a cabin motel across the street from the homesite. We left at about 9:30 a.m. the next day, and arrived at the Little House in the Prairie Museum near Independence, Kan. at about 1 p.m. We toured the homesite for about two hours, then went to Independence, checked into the hotel and played mini-golf at the park. We drove back home the next day.

7. PEPIN, WISCONSIN.
LITTLE HOUSE IN THE BIG WOODS

So of course you want to know more about each homesite. Here is a breakdown of the Little House sites in the Midwest, in the order in which Laura lived in them.

A sign at the marina welcomes you to Pepin.

Laura was born near Pepin, Wis. The town draws in a lot of tourists, and they're not necessarily there for the Laura sites. Situated on Lake Pepin, and nestled by the "Big Woods of Wisconsin," it's a popular spot for outdoor enthusiasts, and it's only an hour-and-a-half drive from Minneapolis.

Laura sites

The Laura Ingalls Wilder Memorial Society, Inc. was established in 1974. The nonprofit group operates the Laura Ingalls Wilder Museum in Pepin, and the log cabin wayside, located about seven miles east of town.

A replica 1800s-style kitchen fills a room in the Laura Ingalls Wilder museum in Pepin, Wis.

Museum

The museum has three large rooms: The center is the gift shop. One room has items pertaining to Laura's time period. The other room has mainly transportation-themed items.

In the "Laura time period" room there are a few items that were owned by Laura as an adult. In a room at the back of the museum

A dress owned by Anna Barry, who was Laura and Mary's first teacher.

is a replica 1800s-style kitchen, with two old stoves, a butter churn and other old kitchen items. Laura went to school while she lived in the Big Woods, although she didn't mention that in the Little House book. The museum has a dress on display that Laura's first teacher owned. A display case houses dolls representing each member of the Ingalls family.

Another section of the museum depicts the town's river and transportation heritage. A covered wagon, and a replica steamboat pilothouse are among the items on display.

Another room off to the side of the "transportation" room is decked out like a school room, with a black board and desks. The museum's entrance opens to the gift store in the building's center. The store offers many Laura and Laura-related items. There are books about Laura and pioneer times. There are sunbonnets and pioneer dresses, plus jewelry and candy.

In a nod to the town's river heritage, the museum displays a partial replica steamboat pilothouse.

For more information about the museum, visit the museum's website: **lauraingallspepin.com**.

The Little House Wayside

Every Little House lover who journeys to Pepin must visit the Little House Wayside log cabin. It's a seven-mile drive on County Road CC, a rural road that seems to go up, up, up from the river at Pepin. The wayside is

The Little House Wayside is located east of Pepin on the land the Ingalls family owned.

located on the land where the Ingalls family actually owned and lived, as Laura described in "Little House in the Big Woods." There is a small gravel parking area. The cabin is a replica of the cabin Laura describes. The outside of the cabin looks the way I pictured the house from the book, except it's no longer surrounded by woods. During the summer, the door to the house is open. When we were there, we found a modern-style picnic table inside, and one side of the house was closed off to make two separate rooms. The outside of the house is perfect for photo opportunities. On the day we visited in mid-July, beautiful flowers grew all around the house, so it was especially picturesque. A large plaque on the land explains the land's significance.

Lake Pepin and the marina

Little House readers know that Laura and Mary gathered pebbles at the lakeshore when they visited town. The lake now has a marina and docks. Along the lake shore there are still plenty of pebbles waiting to be picked up. Just be sure there aren't any holes in your pocket!

Looking toward the marina at Lake Pepin.

How much time you'll spend in and around Pepin

There is no formal tour in the museum, so you're free to spend as much time as you want exploring the museum, and at the wayside. That said, expect to spend at least a half hour looking at the items in the museum, or 45 minutes if you want to spend the time to thoroughly read the signage about the items. If you go to the lakeside and marina you could spend another half hour looking at the lake and picking up pebbles. It takes about 15 minutes to drive to the wayside outside of town. Expect to spend at least a half hour looking at the wayside log cabin and outbuildings, and longer if you want to reflect for a while.

Non-Laura things to see and do

The area offers many outdoor activities including boating, fishing, and kayaking.

Where to eat
In my opinion, this is the best food you'll find at any of the homesite towns. We ate lunch at the Pickle Factory. It's a restaurant/bar. I enjoyed my veggie/cheese melt, and Lindsay liked the grilled cheese. They have an outside balcony that overlooks the lake.

The Harbor View has earned rave reviews on online review sites. We didn't eat there because there was a long line outside the place (a good sign, unless you're really hungry).

Where to stay
There are a few hotels, and a campground in Pepin. There also are several bed and breakfasts. You can also find lodging fairly close by in Minnesota at Wabasha, Lake City, and Red Wing.

How to get there, and expected drive time
Pepin is on the west side of Wisconsin, hugging the Mississippi River. It's pretty much central north to south in the state. Highway 35, the Great River Road, is Pepin's main street. If you're coming from the west, the closest places to cross the river are Red Wing, Minn., from the north, or Wabasha, Minn., from the south. Either way, it's only one lane in either direction, so although it's only 10 miles from Wabasha to Pepin, it feels longer as the speed limit is low, and you can only go as fast as the traffic ahead of you. The drive between Red Wing and Pepin is gorgeous along the River Road. There are huge bluffs to the east, and wonderful views of Lake Pepin and the river to the west.

8. INDEPENDENCE, KANSAS. LITTLE HOUSE ON THE PRAIRIE

In 1869 the Ingalls family moved onto land about 13 miles southwest of Independence, Kansas. They lived there until May 1871. This is the setting of the book "Little House on the Prairie." Highlights from the book include the description of the log cabin, Pa digging a well, and Mr. Edwards crossing the nearby creek to bring Christmas to the family.

The replica log cabin at the Little House on the Prairie Museum.

Little House on the Prairie Museum
The Little House on the Prairie Museum, located on the land on which the Ingalls family actually lived, has a replica log cabin. Both

inside and out, it closely matches the description of the log cabin from the book. It has a handmade table, a small bed plus other handmade items. I expected to see Ma standing in front of the fire cooking rabbit stew. For me, the highlight of the visit was seeing a hand-dug well that is believed to be the one Pa dug with the help of their neighbor. It's amazing to see something that Pa made, and that had a key role in the book.

The museum also includes a one-room schoolhouse and a post office building that the museum had moved from other locations. In both buildings, signs warned us not to cross a rope draped across the room. A very small gift shop has a few items that are unique to this site.

This hand dug well is believed to be the one Laura described Pa digging in the "Little House on the Prairie" book.

The schoolhouse (on the left), and the post office (right) were moved to the museum site from other areas.

For more information, visit the museum's website: **littlehouseontheprairiemuseum.com.**

How much time you'll spend in Independence
There is no guided tour at the museum, so you're

free to go through the buildings at your own pace. We spent about an hour and a half at the museum. During that time we went in and out of each of the buildings several times, taking note of things we'd missed each time. We went through the gift shop and made purchases. We talked with and asked questions of the very knowledgeable museum worker. Plus we took a lot of photos.

I asked the museum worker about the creek that Mr. Edwards crossed so he could bring the Christmas presents to the girls. She pointed out where the creek is – from where we stood in the museum gift shop I could see a grove of trees – but she said the creek is not accessible.

Other area Laura sites
The grave of Dr. Tann, the doctor who likely saved the lives of Laura and her family when they had malaria, is in the Mount Hope Cemetery in Independence.

Non-Laura things to see and do
In Independence, Riverside Park is a really nice 100-acre park. It boasts a mini-golf course (only a dollar a person!) that is themed on sites of the area. There also are playgrounds, a small train that people can ride in for a small fee, a carousel, picnic areas, buildings available for event rental. The park also includes the Ralph Mitchell Zoo, which has a variety of native and exotic animals. The zoo includes a monkey island that was built in the 1930s.

Where to eat
You'll have no trouble finding food. There are a few restaurants, including the usual chain fast food places, in Independence. There also are a few restaurants in Coffeyville to the southeast.

Where to stay
There are a few chain and privately-owned motels in Independence, as well as in nearby Coffeyville.

How to get there, and expected drive time
For a place that's out in the middle of nowhere, finding the homesite was surprisingly easy. If you're coming from Mansfield, the drive takes about three and a half hours. Consult a map, but basically from Mansfield, take Highway 60 west to Interstate 44 west. Take 166/400 west and continue (many miles) to the small town of Tyro, Kan. At Tyro, take County Road 2700 north about six miles, to west on County Road 3000. Watch for the signs.

9. WALNUT GROVE, MINNESOTA. ON THE BANKS OF PLUM CREEK

Laura and her family lived in Walnut Grove, Minn. off and on between 1874 and 1879. And the "Little House" TV show was set in Walnut Grove. These days, drivers entering the town from the east can't miss the huge sign "Welcome to Walnut Grove, childhood home of pioneer author Laura Ingalls Wilder." Each year since 1978 the entire community has come together to celebrate Laura on three weekends in July for the "Fragments of a Dream" pageant. During that time, the community's attention focuses on the pageant. For example, while in a

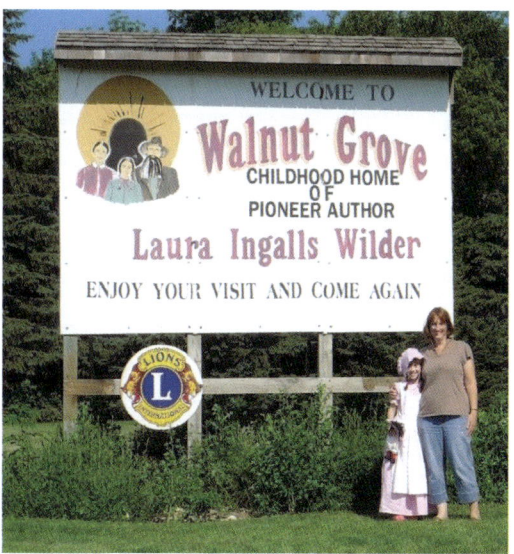

If you're coming from the east, Walnut Grove, Minn. welcomes you as it recognizes Laura's place in the town's history.

convenience store on opening night of the pageant, a man asked me "Are you going to see it?" I knew immediately that he was asking if we were going to the pageant. As it turned out, he and his daughter were performing in the play. He portrayed neighbor Mr. Kennedy, and his daughter had the coveted role of Mary Ingalls. And the next morning, we were in Nellie's Café and overheard local people talking about the opening-night performance.

Laura Ingalls Wilder Museum
The museum has a little bit of everything, all in several buildings. There is no tour guide for the museum so you can explore the buildings for as long as you like. You will receive a brochure when you pay your admission. Be sure to read the brochure as you visit so you don't miss anything, and take your time.
There's a building with a few items that adult Laura and Rose owned. There is a room full of TV show memorabilia, the highlight of which is the actual mantel in the Ingalls' home on the TV show. One building has a room devoted to TV show cast members who have passed away. There is an impressive collection of tiny replicas of buildings from the TV show, some even made of toothpicks. Another building has areas where children (and adults) can pretend that they're shopping in an old-time grocery store. It's complete with an antique cash register, and shelves of old canned goods and other items to buy. There's also an old-time switchboard, and an old-time post office.
For more information about the museum, or anything related to Laura in the town, visit the community's Laura website: **walnutgrove.org**.

Museum gift shop
When you walk into the museum, you find yourself in the gift

shop. In my opinion, this is the best gift shop of any of the museum homesites. You can find everything Laura that you can possibly imagine – plus items you probably didn't think of. They have the Laura water globes and the covered wagon pencil sharpeners that were at most of the other gift shops. But they also offer a plethora of TV show memorabilia, even a canvas bag handmade by the actress who played Miss Beadle on the TV show. There's an entire section of items made for 18-inch dolls, including a doll-size tin lunch pail for less than $2. There is also a section for train enthusiasts. There is absolutely every book about Laura, both fiction and nonfiction. They even have a Laura bobblehead. We bought items here the first day, and came back for more (including the previously-mentioned Charlotte doll) the second day.

"Reflections of a Dream" pageant

If you visit Walnut Grove during the last three weekends in July, you don't want to miss the "Reflections of a Dream" pageant, which depicts Walnut Grove during the Ingalls' time there. Hundreds of community volunteers work to put the show on. There are huge sets, live animals, real fire, and a pond with water.

The "Reflections of a Dream" pageant in Walnut Grove from the front row of the yellow section in 2014.

The Ingalls family and Laura are the central characters, but the pageant also focuses on the people in the town. It reminded me a bit of a live version of the "Little House" TV show. You can buy numbered seat tickets, which are chairs with numbers on them. You can even go to the well-managed and designed website and order the seats yourself. Or you can purchase general admission tickets when you get there. For general admission, you sit on the hillside on your own chair or blanket. Visit walnutgrove.org/seating.htm to find the seating chart.

For the 2014 season Friday night opening show, I called two

months early and ordered front-row yellow section seats. The yellow section is on the right side as you look at the stage. They were good seats, though the view was partially obstructed by the stage lighting poles, an aspect I knew about before I bought the tickets. We liked the pageant so much that we came back the next night. For the second performance, we wanted a different perspective, so I bought general admission seats. We sat on our blankets on the hill behind the numbered seats. We liked watching from farther away, where we could see the entire stage, instead of the area right in front of us. It did get a little chilly though, and sitting on the grass made it seem colder still. We were glad we'd brought plenty of blankets. Perhaps the ideal spot would be in one of the numbered chairs, far back in the center of the audience.

Do note that the pageant doesn't begin until 9 p.m., and ends at about 11 p.m. Factor in the time to get autographs of the performers after the show, or time sitting in traffic waiting to leave the site grounds, and it's a late night – though well worth it.

Festival
In July on pageant Saturdays, the community hosts a family festival in the park in the city's center. There are vendors, activities, and musical and dance performances. Vendors sell all sorts of craft-type items. People sold hand-made jewelry, dish towels with crocheted holders, hand-made blankets, pre-owned toys. A few authors sold autographed copies of their books. For the kids, there were free activities such as sand art, and making corn husk dolls.

Laura and Nellie contest

A main attraction at the festival is the Laura-Nellie Look Alike Contest. Girls age 8 to 12 from all over the country wear pioneer dresses and sunbonnets

The Laura-Nellie Look Alike Contest in Walnut Grove are fun for girls to compete in, and for adults to watch.

and compete in the contests. If your daughter plans to participate, be sure to enter her during the registration time, usually a couple of hours before it begins. Each participant goes onto the stage (an area under a tent) where an emcee asks her questions such as where she's from, and who she came with. Lastly, the Laura entrants are asked a trivia question about Laura, and the Nellie entrants are asked a Nellie-related question. From those entrants, the judges choose four Lauras and four Nellies to plan and perform a short skit together. After the skit performances, the judges choose one Laura and one Nellie winner. The winners receive a small prize.

My daughter loved participating in the contest. It's all good fun.

Plum Creek

The location where Laura lived on Plum Creek is just north of Walnut Grove on Highway 5. The dugout site is my favorite Laura homesite location. The land is now owned by the Gordon family, and the family graciously allows people to drive onto their land and visit Plum Creek. They ask only for a $5 donation per car. There is a drop box as you drive by their house. Once you reach the parking area near the creek, you can walk around the creek area. On the other side of the footbridge, you can stand within feet of the actual location of the Ingalls' dugout. You can wade in Plum Creek and look for crabs and leeches. We did not see any crabs but as I mentioned earlier, we did actually see one leech swimming around upstream from the wading area, so they are still in there. Waders beware!

Seeing the Plum Creek dugout site, and wading in Plum Creek are among the pleasures of visiting Walnut Grove.

Other Laura-related sites

There are several other sites in town that you'll want to see. The bell that Pa helped pay for (instead of buying the boots that he needed so badly), is in the belfry of the English Lutheran Church. On pageant Saturdays, the museum offers a bus tour of sites around the town. During that tour, the guide will ring the church bell. The school where Mary, Laura, and Carrie attended is located at Fourth and Washington, and the Masters Hotel where Laura worked is at Eighth and County Road 20. Both buildings currently are not open for viewing.

The bell that Pa Ingalls helped pay for is currently in the belfry of the English Lutheran Church in Walnut Grove.

Wheels Across the Prairie Museum

About seven miles west in Tracy is the Wheels Across the Prairie Museum, which tells the story of transportation on the Minnesota prairie. Readers of the Little House books will remember that Laura traveled by train with her mother and sisters from Walnut Grove to Tracy in "By the Shores of Silver Lake." According to the museum's website, museum highlights include a four-unit train, and a depot that was moved to the location from Volga, S.D. Visit wheelsacrosstheprairie.org for more information.

Sod House on the Prairie.

Sod houses were very common on the prairie in the late 19th Century. A family has built sod and other pioneer-style homes on their property near Sanborn 18 miles east of Walnut Grove. Paths through the tall prairie grass lead to various buildings, including a prairie soddy, a dugout, and a log cabin. Admission is $4 each person, cash only.

Plan to spend about an hour or less looking through the buildings. Visit sodhouse.org for more information.

How much time to spend in Walnut Grove
You'll want to allow at least a day in Walnut Grove, and if you're there during a festival and pageant, plan to spend at least one night in the area also.

As noted earlier, the museum does not have a guided tour of the buildings. You're free to spend as much time as you'd like. It took a couple of hours for us to go through all the buildings. Although we didn't rush through, there's so much to see, that we didn't see everything. There are several hands-on activities for children, so allow extra time for that if you have kids.

At the Plum Creek dugout site, you can spend 20 minutes if you want to look around and quickly dip your feet in the creek. Or you can spend an hour and a half like we did, and splash and play in the creek, plus walk around the grounds. If you're in the area on a festival day, plan to spend an hour or so looking at vendors' items in the park. Kids will likely want to do the crafts, so allow time for that. The Nellie and Laura contest begins at 3 p.m., and with about 30 entrants, it was over at a little before 5 p.m.

If you attend a pageant, you'll need to plan an entire evening for the event. The pageant begins at 9 p.m., but you'll likely want to arrive early to enjoy the ambience. A local singing group is usually a part of the pre-pageant festivities also.

Non-Laura things to see and do
Plum Creek Park and other nearby areas offer many outdoor

activities, including swimming, boating, nature hike trails, and other camping fun.

Where to eat
There are a few restaurants in Walnut Grove. Nellie's Place serves typical diner food. The Walnut Grove Bar and Grill offers sandwiches, burgers and more. On pageant nights, community groups take turns serving meals in the Walnut Grove Community Center. Hoyt's Convenience has various items including pizza, burritos and sandwiches – all of which you can call and order ahead of time.

Where to stay
This can't be stated enough, if you're planning to be in the area on a pageant weekend, book your lodging or campground early, regardless of where you decide to stay. Keep in mind that the pageant ends at 11 p.m., and that you'll have to drive to your lodging afterward, so it's a good idea to be as close to Walnut Grove as possible.

That said, unfortunately there are no hotels in Walnut Grove. The city park in Walnut Grove has a large campground for both RVs and tents. The sites can be reserved ahead of time. There are several other campgrounds within 30 or so miles away. Visit walnutgrove.org/camping.htm for a list of nearby camping sites.

If you don't want to camp, there is a hotel and a bed and breakfast in Tracy, about 10 miles to the west. There is one hotel about 15 minutes away to the east in Lamberton. There are also chain hotels in Marshall, about 40 minutes to the northwest, and in Mankato an hour and a half away to the east.

How to get there, and expected drive time
Walnut Grove is located on Highway 14 in southwest Minnesota.

The drive from Pepin to Walnut Grove will take about four hours. Highway 14 is one lane for the entire drive from Walnut Grove to De Smet to the west, and that drive will take a little over two hours.

10. BURR OAK, IOWA.
PIONEER GIRL

Although Laura didn't write about it in the Little House books, the Ingalls family lived in Burr Oak in 1876. For a few months, the family lived in, and managed the Masters Hotel, which is now open for tours. Laura did tell about her year in Burr Oak in her manuscript "Pioneer Girl," which was published as a well-received annotated book in 2014. There also is a fictionalized book about her time there, as well as a nonfiction book.

The parlor room in the Masters Hotel in Burr Oak, Iowa looks like it's waiting for weary 19th Century travelers.

Museum

When visiting, you'll buy tickets for the Masters Hotel tour in the visitor center, which is a historic brick bank building that is across the street and to the north of the Masters Hotel. There is a nice gift shop in the visitor center, and restrooms. The visitor center is itself a historic site. It was once a bank, and was famously robbed in the 1930s. Old bank deposit boxes and information about the bank are on display.

Tours of the hotel begin once there are enough people. You walk across the street with the guide to the Masters Hotel. Once you're at the Masters Hotel, the tour guide shows you a short DVD movie about the hotel, and about the Ingalls family. The day we went, the very knowledgeable tour guide gave interesting facts about the Ingalls family, and about the time period, including what it was like to travel in that time. She encouraged us to take photos, even inside the building. The front doors of the hotel, which face the street, open to the main floor. From the outside on the main floor, the hotel doesn't look very big. On the inside it is surprisingly large. The ground slopes in the back of the building, and the lowest level has doors to the outside. That lowest level looks massive.

The room where the Ingalls family lived while they managed the Masters Hotel in Burr Oak, Iowa.

During the tour, you get to see the entire building, including the top level. On the main floor, the one that is street level, there is a "travelers" room, where men met and congregated, a parlor where women and children passed time, and two bedrooms.

You'll also get to see a brick that came from the building where Grace was born.

Upstairs, there are four bedrooms where hotel guests stayed, and a cot at the top of the stairs where the stagecoach driver slept. On the lowest level, you'll see the kitchen where Ma prepared three meals a day for guests. Right next to the kitchen is a bath area, where guests could enjoy a bath for a fee. The lowest level also has a bedroom where the Ingalls family lived while they managed the hotel.

Behind the hotel is a park, and a creek where Laura played so many years ago. Nearby is the cemetery where Laura also spent time when she lived in the town.

For more information about the Laura Ingalls Wilder Park and Museum, visit **lauraingallswilder.us**.

How much time you'll spend in Burr Oak
As previously noted, the tour is guided, so you're not on your own at this museum. The tour of the hotel took about 45 minutes. There is a covered wagon in back of the Masters Hotel for photo opportunities. You can also spend time in the park behind the hotel building, and you can visit the cemetery. Allow at least three hours all together.

Non-Laura things to see and do
The area around Burr Oak abounds with outdoor activities. Canoeing is popular on the Upper Iowa River. A few campgrounds near Decorah offer transportation to a drop spot upriver, then you float back to the campground. Fishing seemed popular. The charming main street in Decorah to the south is lined with

shops and restaurants, and murals painted on the walls. There is a nice bike riding path in Decorah, and you can see a waterfall at Dunning Spring Park. Near the waterfall, there is a park with an ice cave. I'd planned for us to see both waterfall and ice cave, but we ran out of time.

Decorah also has Vesterheim, a Swedish-American Museum, which, according to the museum's website, has the most comprehensive collection of Norwegian-American artifacts in the world. The attraction has numerous buildings.

And in Preston and Lanesboro, Minn. north of Burr Oak, there also are many outdoor activities. There is a long bike trail along the Root River. Tubing, kayaking, and canoeing are available on the river. Many Amish people live in the area (we saw several Amish driving their horse and buggies as we traveled through southeast Minnesota.).

Where to eat

In Burr Oak, there is a bar and grill next door to the Masters Hotel. Decorah has a full range of restaurants, including locally-owned, and chain fast food. To the north, Preston, Minn., and Lanesboro, Minn. also boast local restaurants.

Where to stay

It's ironic that in a town where the Ingalls family ran a hotel, there currently is no lodging. The closest place to Burr Oak to stay overnight is in Decorah, which is about 20 minutes south. There are a few chain motels in Decorah. There also is a city-run campground, plus a couple of privately-owned campgrounds outside of town. All of the campgrounds are next to the beautiful Upper Iowa River. If you're heading north to Pepin, Spring Valley, or Walnut Grove after your Burr Oak visit, you may consider staying in Lanesboro or Preston, Minn. about 30 minutes to the north. Both Preston and Lanesboro towns have bed and breakfasts as well as campgrounds on and near the Root River. My research found the campgrounds in southeastern Minnesota to be more expensive than in Decorah, but still much less than staying in a hotel.

How to get there, and expected drive time
Finding Burr Oak is simple, but like all of the sites, it's not near any large highways. You can get there by taking Iowa state highway 52 from the north or south. It is about a two-hour drive from Pepin. The area surrounding Burr Oak is beautiful, with green rolling hills and many creeks and rivers. This site is definitely worth the time if you can fit it into your travel schedule.

11. DE SMET, SOUTH DAKOTA.
BY THE SHORES OF SILVER LAKE, THE LONG WINTER, LITTLE TOWN ON THE PRAIRIE, THESE HAPPY GOLDEN YEARS, THE FIRST FOUR YEARS

Laura spent nearly 15 years living in and around De Smet. That makes for a lot to see in this town.

Laura Ingalls Wilder Historic Homes
The nonprofit Laura Ingalls Wilder Memorial Society has a guided tour of four buildings. The society also operates the

The Surveyor's House that Laura describes in vivid detail in "By the Shores of Silver Lake" looks just as described.

gift shop, an exhibition room, plus a discovery building that has hands-on activities. For the guided tour, you walk with your tour guide and other tour guests, from one building to the next. The tour begins at the Surveyor's House – yes, the actual house that is described in detail in "By the Shores of Silver Lake." The building was moved from its original location outside of town, to next door to the visitor center. It is restored to look just as Laura described it in the book. You see the stairs leading to the attic bedroom, and the pantry where Laura found an abundance of food that included canned food, pickles, and crackers. Unfortunately, they don't allow visitors to take photos inside the Surveyors house, and they don't allow visitors to go into the second level.

The replica prairie schoolhouse is modeled after the Brewster Schoolhouse in which Laura taught her first session of school. Guests sit in the desks while the tour guide provides details about what it was like to teach and go to school on the prairie when Laura taught. The one-room building is small, the way an actual prairie schoolhouse would have been. It looks very close to the way Garth Williams illustrated it.

Also on the tour is the First School of De Smet, the actual schoolhouse where Laura and Carrie attended school. Yes, this is the schoolhouse where Laura battled with her teacher Eliza Jane Wilder in "Little Town on the Prairie." The society purchased the building, moved it to its present location, and restored it. During the restoration, they discovered the blackboard had been drawn on by school children of long ago. To preserve the chalk masterpieces, the museum covered the blackboard with clear plastic. To help set the mood, there are slates on the desks that have sayings from the "Little Town on the Prairie" book. The "Lousy, Lizy Jane" poem is on quite a few of them.

The last building on the guided tour is the Ingalls Home on Third Street, the house in which Pa, Ma, and Mary lived out their lives. Pa built the house in 1887 after the Ingalls family moved from the homestead. Do note that it is several blocks from the location of the other buildings, so you'll drive there in your own car. After the tour group reassembles at the house, the guide will take you into the house and give details about the house.

The house has two stories, and is made of lumbered wood. The society has restored the house to look as close as possible to the way it looked when the Ingalls lived there. Before letting us loose to look through the house on our own, the tour guide showed us photos of Ma and Mary that were taken in the house. The organization did a wonderful job restoring the house. It was amazing to look at a photo, and then look around the house and "see" the photo come to life.

Caroline Ingalls' room in Ingalls Home on Third Street, the last home built by Charles Ingalls, where Pa, Ma, and Mary lived out their lives.

My favorite item in the house was "Pa's big green book." It is the actual book that Laura and family members look at in a few of the Little House books. It was very fun to see it in person, and to imagine Laura and Mary looking through it with their cousins on Christmas in the Big Woods. Be sure to look closely in Mary's room on the first floor. Items of note are family items in the dresser drawers. Also, a letter written by Eliza Jane Wilder was printed in a newspaper that was used as insulation in the wall.

Once you're finished looking at the lower level, you can walk upstairs to the second floor. There you can see restored bedrooms. The organization also gives out free tour maps that will show you additional places of interest for a self-guided tour.

The gift shop has a nice assortment of Laura items for sale.

For more information about the Laura Ingalls Wilder Historic Home Tours, visit **discoverlaura.org**.

Ingalls Homestead

Also in De Smet, you'll want to visit the Ingalls Homestead. It is a privately-owned and operated living history attraction located on the land that the Ingalls family homesteaded for five years. Both Lindsay and I loved this place. There are multiple buildings, each depicting life on the prairie. There is a replica dugout. There also is a replica claim shanty, much like the one that the Ingalls family first lived in when they homesteaded the land. Ma's House is a replica of the house the Ingalls family lived in on the homestead after they had built onto the claim shanty.

Ma's House at the Ingalls Homestead in De Smet. The house is a replica of the home the Ingalls built on their homestead. Just like the Ingalls' home, a ring of cottonwood trees surrounds the house.

At the homestead, there are many hands-on activities. Lindsay loved operating an antique pedal sewing machine, and washing laundry with a washboard and wringer washer. I practically had to drag her away from those activities.

You also can make a corn cob doll just like Laura's Susan. Have you ever wondered about grinding wheat in a coffee mill, like the Ingalls family did during the long winter? Here's your chance to find out how hard it is. And if you've read "The Long Winter" and were never sure how they twisted the hay to make those hay sticks, this is your chance to try

Doing laundry (top photo), and twisting hay (bottom photo), are two of the many hands-on activities you can do at Ingalls Homestead in De Smet.

making one yourself. They have a sled full of hay, and a worker to teach you how to twist the hay. You can pump a working water well. There is a horse or mule wagon ride that takes you to the school house. Kids even get to take turns at the reins. Once at the school house, a teacher gives a lesson on what it was like for children to attend a prairie schoolhouse, and teachers to teach at a prairie schoolhouse.

As previously mentioned, you can spend the night in a covered wagon at Ingalls Homestead. They of course are not real covered wagons. Instead, they are like small lodges covered with a hard, fiberglass-like top that looks like a wagon, and they have non-moving wheels. Each has a bed at the far end, seats with storage on the side, and electricity. There is no bathroom in the wagons, so in that respect, it's like camping (makes it more authentic that way!). There also is one bunk house that can be reserved. The homestead also has RV parking spots, or you can pitch a tent. If you want to stay in a wagon, or the bunkhouse, be sure to make your reservation early – especially if you'll be there on a pageant night. They do book up quickly.

At Ingalls Homestead, you can spend the night in a covered wagon.

Check the Ingalls Homestead website for more information, at **ingallshomestead.com**.

Pageant
The Laura Ingalls Wilder Pageant Society performs a pageant on the last three Friday, Saturday, and Sundays of July on land next to the Ingalls Homestead. The pageant tells the story of one of the Little House books that took place in De Smet. In 2015 they

started over with the books, and told the story of "By the Shores of Silver Lake." Next was "The Long Winter," and so on. All of the seating is general admission. You can sit on their benches, or bring your own chairs or blanket. Be sure to arrive early to enjoy the activities before the pageant begins. The year we were there, activities included free mule-drawn wagon rides, face painting, and coloring pages. When we were there they chose a few kids out of the audience to sing a song during the pageant. Words to a song were printed in the newspaper-sized program, and the audience was encouraged to sing along as well. The pageant begins at 8 p.m. so you'll see the sun setting over the prairie during the pageant. Beautiful. The pageant ended a little after 9 p.m. Be sure to take blankets. Evenings are chilly on the prairie.

Visit **desmetpageant.org** for more information.

The pageant at De Smet takes place adjacent to the prairie land where the Ingalls family homesteaded.

Amount of time to spend in De Smet

Plan to spend at least a full day in De Smet. Though to see all of the Laura sites in and around town, plus the tour and time at the Ingalls Homestead you will need a day and a half. You should plan on an hour and a half minimum for the museum's guided tour of the buildings. If you have children, they'll want to do the activities in the museum's Discovery Center, so allow about a half-hour to an hour for that. To really see the exhibition in the main building, you would need at least an hour.

You'll want to spend at least half a day at Ingalls Homestead, and you can easily spend the entire day there if you have kids. If you attend the pageant, you'll need to allow a couple of hours for that as well, and probably stay in the area for the night.

Other area Laura sites
In addition to the museum and the homestead, there are many Laura sites to see in and around De Smet. You can drive to the land where Laura and Almanzo homesteaded, you can shop in Loftus Store, which is still in its original location, you can see the Ingalls Store site. In the De Smet Cemetery, you can see the gravestones of Ma, Pa, Mary, Carrie, and Grace, plus many other people mentioned in the books, including Mr. and Mrs. Loftus, Mr. and Mrs. Boast, and C.S. G. Fuller, who owned Fuller Hardware which was often mentioned in "The Long Winter."

Non-Laura things to see and do
Forty miles to the east, Brookings has a children's museum. The city of Sioux Falls is an hour and a half away. The city offers a variety of attractions including seeing Sioux Falls at Falls Park, the Sertoma Butterfly House & Marine Cove, the Great Plains Zoo and Delbridge Museum of Natural History. Plus, learn more about history at the Pettigrew Home and Museum, and at the Old Courthouse Museum.

Where to eat
There is one chain sandwich place, a couple of local restaurants, and a grocery/bakery.

Where to stay

There are a few motels and bed and breakfasts in De Smet, as well as the aforementioned Ingalls Homestead, and a couple of campgrounds, including the city-run campground.

How to get there, and expected drive time

De Smet is on Highway 14, about 45 minutes west of Brookings, S.D. , and 30 minutes east of Huron, S.D. Highway 14 is about an hour north of Interstate 90. It takes about two hours to travel between De Smet and Walnut Grove on Highway 14.

12. MANSFIELD, MISSOURI. WHERE THE LITTLE HOUSE BOOKS WERE WRITTEN

What you'll see

At the Laura Ingalls Wilder Historic Home and Museum, you'll see where Laura and Almanzo lived most of their lives, and where Laura wrote the Little House series. You'll also see a wealth of items (yes, the actual items!) that were mentioned in the books. There also are photos, and many items that were owned and even made by Laura when she was an adult, and there are many items owned and made by daughter Rose Wilder Lane.

Laura and Almanzo built the farmhouse at Rocky Ridge using materials from the farm.

Some background. Traveling in a modified buggy, Laura, Almanzo, and their daughter Rose left De Smet, S.D. and headed south in

1894. They stopped traveling when they reached Mansfield, Mo. They bought land and named it Rocky Ridge Farm. Over the years Laura and Almanzo built their beautiful Farmhouse from materials on the land. In 1928 when she was enjoying success as a writer, Rose built her parents a more modern house that was dubbed the "Rock House." Laura and Almanzo lived in the Rock House from 1928 to 1936, while Rose lived in the Farmhouse. Laura wrote the first four books in the Little House series in the Rock House. She wrote the last four, plus presumably the manuscript for "The First Four Years" in the Farmhouse.

In order to preserve the homes and personal items, Rose and a friend established the Wilder Home Association after Laura's death in 1957. Today, visitors are able to tour both houses, plus see many of Laura's personal items, in a museum just downhill from the Farmhouse. One note, you can take photos of the outside of the buildings, but no photos are allowed inside any of the buildings.

Highlights in the museum are Pa's fiddle, the little china jewel-box that Laura received as a Christmas gift in "On the Banks of Plum Creek," and Laura and Mary's slates. Name cards mentioned in "Little Town on the Prairie" are on display. You'll see many photos, plus dresses that Laura wore as an adult.

The Farmhouse tour begins in the kitchen. Going through each room of the house, the guide will share interesting facts, and also give you plenty of time to look through the house on your own with the help of a brochure. In the kitchen, note the set of small stairs that go up to a second level. The stairs lead to what was once Rose's room when she was a little girl. In the bedroom, even the items on the dresser have been left as they were when Laura died. In the parlor, you'll see Laura's writing desk. This is the actual desk at which Laura wrote the Little House books. Moving into the living room at the front of the house, note the fireplace, which Laura and Almanzo built using rocks from the property. Also note the carpentry work in the book cases and the staircase. You'll also want to look for Almanzo's cane.

There is a pathway between the Farmhouse and the Rock House. For the past couple of years it has been closed while the association reconstructs it. If it's not open, you'll drive about a half-mile east to visit the Rock House. Like the Farmhouse, the Rock House has been restored meticulously to the way it looked when Laura and Almanzo lived there. The house has warm yellow paint, and a Mediterranean feel.

Rose Wilder Lane had the Rock House built for her parents in 1928 for the then extravagant price of $12,000.

Outside, be sure to see the heirloom garden, and the chicken coop with heirloom chickens. Laura was well-known for her knowledge of caring for laying hens.

The gift shop is good, with plenty of books and Laura souvenir items. For only a dollar or so you can buy a reprint of a local newspaper that includes articles of local people talking about what they remember of the Wilders. The store also sells a charming print illustration of the Ingalls family.

The museum in Mansfield honors Laura's chicken-raising knowledge with a chicken coop that houses the same heritage chicken breeds that Laura raised.

Expected time to spend in Mansfield
To see everything in the museum takes at least an hour and a half. The house tours take about a half hour each for the guides to explain everything. You can then stay longer to look around. Overall, you need at least three hours at this site.

For more information, visit the museum's website: **lauraingallswilderhome.com**.

Other Laura things to see and do
The town square has a small memorial devoted to Laura Ingalls Wilder. Also, Laura, Almanzo, and Rose are buried in the town cemetery.

In July and September, the Ozarks Mountain Players perform a Laura Ingalls Wilder pageant in Mansfield. Visit **laurasmemories.com** for more information.

Non-Laura sights to see
Only about 10 minutes north of Mansfield off Highway 5, you'll find Baker Creek Heirloom Seeds. The family-owned seed business has a huge selection of heritage vegetable, flower, and herb seeds. In addition, they have a village that looks very similar to Walnut Grove from the "Little House on the Prairie" TV show. On summer weekdays, they serve a delicious vegan lunch, and they host a Spring Planting Festival in early spring. They are located about 10 minutes off Highway 5 on the gravel Baker Creek Road. Check their website for more information: rareseeds.com.

The village at Baker Creek Heirloom Seeds resembles Walnut Grove in the "Little House" TV show.

Mansfield is about an hour and a half northeast of Branson, Mo. The popular tourist destination offers many entertainment options, including the Silver Dollar City amusement park, a huge variety of musical shows, and a Titanic museum. Southwest Missouri also abounds with outdoor recreational activities including fishing and boating.

Where to eat
Mansfield has a nice selection of places to eat. There is a chain sandwich restaurant, plus a few locally-owned restaurants that are very good including a pizza place, a Mexican place, and a diner. About 10 miles away in Ava to the south, and Mountain Grove to the east, you'll find more restaurants as well.

Where to stay
There are a few lodging options in Mansfield. The upper level of a historic building in the town square has been restored into a bed and breakfast, and a coffee house downstairs. Across the highway from the museum is a cabin and camping option. About 20 minutes south in Ava there are a few chain hotels. About 20 minutes west in Seymour is a hotel. About an hour north in Lebanon, are several chain hotels. Springfield, Mo. is about 45 minutes to the west and offers many hotels.

How to get there, and expected drive time
Mansfield is on Highway 60 about 45 miles east of Springfield, Mo. I have found that if you're coming from the northeast, the best route is Highway 44 west to Highway 5 south from Lebanon. Both times we've taken this route, there was little traffic on Highway 5, and it's a pretty drive.

12. OTHER SITES OF INTEREST

As mentioned earlier, there are a few Laura-related sites we have not visited. Here is brief information on those sites.

The Almanzo & Laura Ingalls Wilder Association operates Wilder Homestead, the childhood home of Almanzo. It's in upper New York state, near Malone. According to the organization's website, the site includes 84 acres of farmland, the restored house, and reconstructed barns and outbuildings. This is the place that Laura described so vividly in the "Farmer Boy" book. Visit almanzowilderfarm.com for more information.

In the northern Midwest, you can visit Spring Valley, Minn. Laura, Almanzo, and Rose lived on the Wilder farm in Spring Valley from 1890 to 1891 while recovering from hardships. The Spring Valley Methodist Church Museum offers tours of the church, where the Wilder Family were members. Historical items are in the church basement. The grave of Almanzo Wilder's brother Royal is in the town cemetery. Spring Valley is located south of Rochester on Highway 63. Visit springvalleymnmuseum.org for more information.

Laura's sister Mary Ingalls attended what was then called the Iowa College for the Blind, in Vinton. The college still exists and is located at 1002 G Avenue. A plaque near the college notes that Mary attended there. Vinton is about two hours and 15 minutes southwest of Burr Oak.

13. TIPS FOR A GREAT LITTLE HOUSE TRIP

Here are my suggestions to help your trip be the best it can be.

If camping, you'll of course need all your camping equipment plus toiletries, towels and bedding.

Bring maps. Print a map of each town you'll visit, or have it downloaded on your electronic device. Yes, the towns are small, and yes you likely have a GPS and maps on your phone and tablet. But the towns can be more difficult to navigate than you think, and access to the Internet is spotty.

Also take a map to help you get from one town to the next. Again, Internet access isn't always available so it's best to have printed or downloaded maps, and directions that tell you how to get from here to there.

Bring books on CD. A Little House tour will involve some driving, so bring entertainment for the drive. I borrowed audio books from the library that both of us enjoyed listening to. We especially loved listening to the "Julie" American Girl books. In the books, Julie even talks about loving "Little House" and Laura Ingalls Wilder, and she has an adventure on a wagon train. Listening to books entertained both of us as we drove toward our own Little

House adventure.

Bring plenty of snacks and bottled water, for those times when you're in between towns.

Bring blankets. Even during the summer, the prairie gets cool in the evening. You'll especially appreciate blankets during the pageants in Walnut Grove and De Smet.

Bring at least one pair of pants and a jacket, even during the summer.

Bring this guide book (of course!).

Plan non-Laura fun into the trip. Sure, you want to immerse yourself in the pioneer life on this trip, but that doesn't mean you can't have some modern fun too.

Most importantly, bring your sense of adventure!

Website addresses for the main homesites:

Pepin, Wis.: lauraingallspepin.com

Independence, Kan.: littlehouseontheprairiemuseum.com

Walnut Grove, Minn.: walnutgrove.org

Burr Oak, Iowa: lauraingallswilder.us

De Smet, S.D.: discoverlaura.org; ingallshomestead.com

Mansfield, Mo.: lauraingallswilderhome.com

Malone, N.Y.: almanzowilderfarm.com

ABOUT THE AUTHOR

Gina Parsons is an avid "Little House" lover. She has written for newspapers, magazines, and websites. She was a reporter and managing editor for a weekly newspaper, and a writer and editor for a regional parenting magazine. She lives near St. Louis, Mo. She and her daughter are busy planning their next Little House trip.

Email: gparsons.writer@gmail.com
Facebook: @GinaParsonsWriter

Printed in Great Britain
by Amazon